THE IRRESPONSIBLE MAGICIAN

Published by Semiotext(e)
PO BOX 629, South Pasadena, CA 91031
www.semiotexte.com

Thank you Michel Auder, Wayne Koestenbaum, Jim Supanick, Jason Livingston, Paige Sarlin, Leighton Pierce, Peggy Leggat, Rachel Posner, Laska Jimsen, Ivone Margulies, Robert Beavers, Jasmine Moorhead, Matilda Cantwell, Justin Yockel, Miciah Hussey, Marlon Fuentes, Vincent Crapanzano, Phillip Lopate, Jane Brailove Rutkoff, Peter Rutkoff and Sylvia Rutkoff.

Grateful acknowledgment is made to reprint from the following publications: *Animal Shelter*, *Fence Magazine*, *Interval(le)s*, *Satellite Telephone*, *The Coming Envelope*, and *World Picture Journal*.

All artwork by Rebekah Rutkoff unless credited otherwise.

Cover Art: Pierre La Police
www.pierrelapolice.com

Design: Hedi El Kholti

ISBN: 978-1-58435-173-3
Distributed by The MIT Press, Cambridge, Mass. and London, England
Printed in Korea by WeSP through Four Colour Print Group

THE IRRESPONSIBLE MAGICIAN

ESSAYS AND FICTIONS

Rebekah Rutkoff

semiotext(e)

Contents

To Joshua Rutkoff

and in memory of Dara Greenwald

PART ONE

ART IN THE FAMILY

Pleated lamp, private home, New York, NY.

1.

TRANSCRIPT OF AN UN-MADE VIDEO

Were poetics or architecture the root of your salvation?

Poetics.

And when the coral-colored leatherette banquette stuck to the backs of your legs, did you mind?

No.

And when you had to choose between re-creating or cleaning out, which, in general, did you choose?

Cleaning out—starting over.

What pictures did you make first?

Rainbows and suns with long rays, tall ice cream cones, and houses with distinct roofs and receding bushes.

The first painting came easily: it was white over cobalt and there was the smallest amount of orange, with a sibling of vomit green, which streaked its way into the white accidentally. I've never been able to use such a small amount of color within a white ground since then. In fact every painting after that one became difficult. I often got distracted by the motion of the brush—I painted lines that felt nice to make, arcs and arabesques, but that looked terribly ugly on paper. Imagine loading a brush with paint and then making the shape of something close to the old-fashioned number three, the one with a 45 degree angle on top—the combined roundness and points, and the satisfaction of the directional changes. I never learned to exit this scenario: each time I began by using the brush as if it were made to bring pleasure, and each time the results were disastrous.

And drawing?

Drawing was easy and hard. My first drawing teacher had been physically abusive to his wife who taught Caribbean literature and he died suddenly in his early forties. But with him I discovered my need to mimic Jim Dine. I didn't mimic his work per se, but rather some aspect of his combined project and aura. I began by making a series of Jim Dine signatures, and they essentially provided a solution to the painting problem I mentioned earlier in that I could make lines that I enjoyed producing, in terms of a physical sensation, because I have very easy control over strokes, like Jim does, without the pressure of making anything, both because I was copying something, so there was a model, and I was copying writing, so I wasn't making a drawing, and I was making Jim Dine, so in the end I was making something. His work has never made sense to me—it doesn't particularly look like art, largely because of those etchings of hearts, which strike me as absurd, sort of like an orthopedic surgeon's garden. This dilemma of wanting work to look like art is ongoing.

I like to draw women, and you'll notice this is common for the casual drawer—the making of forms of the artist's own gender. I draw women with tiny waists and extreme eyelashes and checkmark noses as fast as possible. And Lisa Yuskavage's women are just painted enlargements of this phenomenon—the globes for breasts and the arched backs and frosty auras—and I'd prefer it if we could say, "paint makes particular room for acknowledgement of this fantasy" rather than "these pictures are important and valuable and rare." I think returning to the most literal understanding of "pictorial" would be helpful—if we're dealing with a picture of language, we should just call it that.

There's a documentary about Jim Dine's preparations for a show in Berlin or Cologne, and in the shots of him making wall drawings, you're watching an identity wondering if it has limits and finding out that the answer is: "no." The creative work is protected by the speed, as a way of breaking the mind's control, but the downside is that you're simply submitting to the authority of another god. Unfortunately my own work seemed to come exclusively from the space halfway between speed and total mind, and I don't see a lot of evidence that good work can come out of that place. But the experience of dilation was compelling and pleasant enough for me to remain there in spite of failure.

And photography?

I spent about a year taking pictures of phallic symbols and then I saw that that was not interesting, so I began to work with color and tried to simply take a picture when I wanted to. In the end my best pictures came from days when I went to museums, because I would find myself walking on fancy avenues I'm not normally on, and I'd pass by these beautifully put together and really well-lit window displays and I'd take three steps and shoot and walk another three steps and shoot and then I'd have a roll of pretty pictures of stacks of cashmere scarves and arrangements of beaded handbags. I also started taking the camera into the bathroom with me at shows. I first did this at a Serra show at Gagosian—the *Torqued Ellipses* were there and I felt so irrelevant and turned on that I walked into the bathroom and took off my pants and took a picture of myself in the mirror without thinking about it. I remember exactly what I was wearing that day—jeans and a lilac-colored, short sleeve angora cardigan sweater. I did the same thing at the Matthew Barney show at the Guggenheim—there's a bathroom about every 500 steps as you're climbing the spiral and I took a photo of the place where the toilet meets the caulking in each one. I remember I had a fever that day, and it was also the afternoon of the Puerto Rican Day Parade along 5th Avenue, and the combination of those things made the show completely intolerable.

And film?

Film was much too complex. I began with animation, which one should never do, and loading film at the stand in the dark caused me deep anxiety. I would sweat through all my clothes. Getting the film to engage and advance seemed such an unlikely possibility that by the time I was ready to shoot all my energy was gone. I did a very meticulous series of my entire sticker collection and another one in which I floated small plastic squares in milk and built miniature worlds inside colored Celestial Seasonings tea tins, but I never looked at any of the footage when I got it back from the lab.

And video?

I noticed that subtly squeezing the nose down the bridge and then allowing the nostrils to slightly flare at the tips, so that the entire nasal enterprise is molded but held quite still—that this in combination with a movement centered on the lips and mouth was essentially a seductive presentation of femininity and a form of masturbation. You'll notice people like Kathie Lee Gifford exploit this technique with great success. When you have the sense that someone is looking at your mouth move, your entire body fits itself into that orifice. Something similar happens when you use the muscles in your lips and lift them just a hair in relationship to the teeth—so that more tooth is exposed.

So I began to tape myself using this technique and I had no success. Essentially the masturbatory aspect took over and I could not control the artwork and my body at the same time.

And Rosalind Krauss?

I had only seen Ros in pictures in which she had the hair in the face and a very severe beauty (there's that famous photo where she's leaning over her typewriter from 1969) so when she came walking down the hall I was frightened. The combination of her stroke and facelift left her looking shiny and disheveled, and over the course of several weeks she proved thoroughly unfit to teach. We were studying Barthes' last lectures on the neutral, and Richard Howard came in to talk about their friendship. I had never heard of Richard Howard before, but he wore a very expensive-looking pastel shirt and oversized tortoise glasses, and by the time he left, he mentioned having translated Gide, Camus, Robbe-Grillet, and Stendhal, so I got the idea that he was important. Philippe Sollers came in too, and I remember a very particular sense of shock that comes from beholding the down-slope of cerebral overwork—the way that casual conversation becomes a charged form, more satisfying, for me, than the written output because you get the primal combination of common sense and left-overs from study. In both instances Ros chastised us after their visits—we hadn't thanked them for their time by asking the proper questions.

And Philip Roth?

Philip Roth was seated in a corner booth at the Russian Samovar with Joyce Carol Oates, whom I've seen a number of times in Theater District restaurants. She left, and he stayed, and moved up to a front table and held court with some apricot-infused vodka. It was essentially a come-sit-on-Santa's-lap situation, and everyone, mostly the young women, took turns.

And Bill Eggleston?

I met Bill Eggleston in the back office of Southside Gallery in Oxford. He was drunk and asked me to sit on his lap and said he hated big breasts. Later we sat on the stoop outside and shared vodka. His mistress Leigh was an alcoholic anorexic. She had a glossy face, stick legs and hardly any eyebrows. She told a sad story about forgetting to use her beauty when she was young.

And Peter Galassi?

Peter Galassi was tall, and he had his hand on the smalls of quite a few women's backs.

And Ed Harris?

Ed Harris was at the bar at the Jackson Pollock opening at MoMA. Amy Madigan was hovering around, waiting for him.

We smoked a cigarette and he asked me why the bar looked the way it did. It was rough silver with lines in it—scratches without grooves. It was a question without a purpose, but I answered it despite not knowing the answer as a way of telling him I would neither acknowledge that I knew he was Ed Harris nor let him dominate me completely if we ever happened to have sex.

And Haskell Wexler?

I love *Medium Cool* and I was surprised that Haskell had so many sports cars, but he's gentle, and you sort of forgive his tasteless relationship to his wealth because you hope it's just an accident.

And William Bennett?

Bill Bennett was at the bar at the Fairmont Miramar in Santa Monica drinking martinis next to the potted tropical plants. He was no longer the Drug Czar at this point. He was using his cell phone and saying, "Hi, it's Billy" loudly. It was rather off-putting. I was staying at the hotel and using it as an interview location to talk to Duane "Dog" Chapman and his wife Beth for a CourtTV documentary. They were the tannest people I'd ever seen.

And Alicia Silverstone?

Alicia Silverstone was terrific. She had bad skin but quite a glow. Apparently she's a vegan.

And Rob Lowe?

Rob Lowe was campaigning for Dukakis in my hometown. I was in high school and wore a purple and metallic scarf in my hair. Later he came by the local pizza place and when I met him, I grabbed onto his hand and held on until he said, "please let go."

And Peter Eisenman?

Peter Eisenman was fine, disappointing and enthralling all at once. He was peaking—he had just finished the grotesque pastel-colored convention center in Columbus—and he gave a giddy lecture about his published letter-writing exercises with Derrida. His son was a noted DJ at my college, so the whole thing added up to an event of sorts. I tried to ask him a question afterwards but he wasn't particularly interested in answering. A few years later I rented a room from a woman in Strasbourg who had worked at Eisenman's studio in New York. She said his home TV was always turned to muted cable porn. She rode a motorcycle and was irritated by my meekness and poor French.

And Louise Bourgeois?

Louise was as you'd expect. She wore small gold hoop earrings and there was a general smell of urine in the house. She served Campari and dirty grapes and she kept using the word "compensation." She looked at my work; she didn't seem to like it much and said it was mysterious. An artist from Paris stopped by—actually he was Swiss, living in Paris, and he had just landed in New York and took a cab straight to Louise's apartment from the airport. He was very muscular, and he came carrying an enormous tube. It was very dramatic: he tapped the tube and removed its contents and unrolled a large sheet on the wall, and it turned out to be a monster-sized photo of Joseph Beuys. All of this was his way of asking if Louise would sit for a similar photo. She thought about it for a moment, and then said yes.

And Aunt Sylvia?

Her paintings are huge, and many of them are bumpy and built up with sand or just paint. She's good with white and cream next to each other, and also with silver and the occasional neon.

And so you finally gave up on being an artist and started video-taping yourself writing?

Yes. I always liked watching women in administrative positions filling out forms: first, there's a kind of direct access that's unusual—you get to stare at this hand at work across from you or below you, and there's generally some kind of extreme competence or at least unwavering convention—the paper is at an angle, it's on a clipboard, and the writing happens at a very regular pace—imagine the cursive being formed, the female script, the humps of the m's and the going back to the t's and i's with a sense of certainty. Of course if there are long nails or draping bracelets, the whole spectacle becomes even better. So I began taping myself filling out forms wearing press-on nails and using high quality pens. Some day I may even make drawings in the margins if it seems right.

Erich Maria Remarque's signature on a window, Osnabrück, Germany.

2.

LOSS OF LUSTER:

A CATALOG OF LUXURIES & ERRORS

1. CHILDREN

In the early eighties Mary Boone refused to represent my great aunt, an abstract painter who works mostly in acrylics, after she learned that Sylvia perceived an amorphous blue spot in one of her own paintings as a female figure. "I don't do representational," Mary said. As a young woman Sylvia and Mark Rothko taught in adjacent classrooms, and when he felt fragile or started to cry, she'd take over his class. At thirty she became a patient of the Hungarian anthropologist and psychoanalyst Geza Roheim in order to unravel her conflicted feelings about having a child. One afternoon she recalled a dream about dropping a large terra cotta vessel. What color is terra cotta? Roheim pressed. Flesh-colored, Sylvia said. The doctor pronounced the analysis complete: the flesh-colored vessel was a burdensome baby, and Sylvia clearly did not want to be a mother.

Sylvia continued to paint, drawn to metallic colors and encaustic for texture, and regretted never having had a child. Years later Roheim wrote about Sylvia's analysis in *Magic and Schizophrenia*, his study of the life-long use of magic to assert infantile control in both primitive societies and coital settings. I brought Roheim's yellow book to Maplewood just before Sylvia's 90th birthday and she read her own case study for the first time. "The analysis revealed that her painting had an anal meaning (smearing) for her, and that the brush was a penis. She had many Lesbian dreams, mostly with herself in the active role. Her first reaction to this awareness was 'Well then I should not paint. I don't want to be a Lesbian.'" Sylvia looked up from the book. "This is bullshit," she said, and stopped reading.

2. CHAGALL

A second great aunt Sylvia was married to the late Uncle Bob, a jeweler who loved argyle sweaters, forgot to keep his eyes on the company ledgers and lost the family fortune in 1952. Sylvia and Bob downgraded to a modest Long Island rental ranch, but they continued to serve smoked fish and German chocolate cake to guests, and managed to hold on to their favorite objects: an orange modernist coffee table, a collection of glass paperweights, a Raphael Soyer charcoal nude and, until they had to trade it in for a nursing home a decade later, a steel blue Chagall bride, floating away from a shtetl in her husband's cloudy embrace. Uncle Bob lost the jewelry business but he kept a stash of chipped gemstones in the den. When I visited, he'd present me with a silk-lined box of once semi- but now non-precious bits and pieces: a tiger-eyed opal, a garnet, an aquamarine.

3. CHRIST

For seven years I was the victim of an unfortunate therapeutic mis-match with a non-Jew. She was blonde and ladylike in her soft suits, shearling jackets and oversized jewels and she didn't let Jesus get in the way of her sophistication. She was Catholic, and she was also going through menopause. Sometimes she turned bright pink during sessions and opened all the windows with passionate haste.

Each fall she returned from the August recess with a new object from her missionary work in exotic locales—she skipped Truro in favor of other commitments. A green lacquer vase filled with miniature buds from her penthouse roof rose garden appeared after her trip to China. I found one of her church's newsletters online, and learned that she once invited the Jesuits over after Mass to smell the roses.

She was offended by my dreams—in one just after 9-11, a giant naked terrorist took the place of the Statue of Liberty. He was painted green and held one hand daintily over his genitals and the other over his mouth in mock shame, and she asked me never to undermine her authority like that again.

But I was impressed by her vibrant femininity and good works, and I tried to open myself to her and the Christian way: at Christmas I submerged gilded ornaments into containers of yogurt with fruit on the bottom until the jam got pushed to the surface, and at Easter I sliced open eggs to assess the fillings. Unfortunately this was of no use. We were unable to bond, and we finally parted ways.

4. CINEMATOGRAPHY

In a dream I was lost in Malibu with my mother. We arrived at a fork, uncertain as to whether to take the road that led to the filmmaker Haskell Wexler's house. We decided against it; we were terribly hungry and realized that once we reached Haskell's home and admired his velvet screening room, tropical landscaping and convertible, reservations would have to be made, and then once at the restaurant, the dissemination of menus and the unfolding of napkins on laps would move the clock even further forward: it would take far too long to reach the moment of food. So we did not choose the filmmaker's exit; instead, we sat in a parked car on Main Street, and ate out of plastic cups: cream colored balls (the color and consistency of marzipan) decorated with a single cherry on top. Much faster than lunch with Haskell Wexler! We were so close to paradise in that parked car—only an automobile's metal skin away from the fresh air and clean money of Malibu. And the car was warm inside, so it was almost like being at the beach.

5. THE CHEF

I had selected the chef from an online singles bazaar and after two brief barstool dates accepted his invitation to come over for reheated Indian food. He drew my attention to a compact box of flatware on the counter (his silver-plated utensils were in storage, in Texas with his mother, but he had found this temporary set while antiquing up the Hudson) and to his kitchen walls, newly painted chalkboard black. He felt conflicted about what sort of markings to make on them. Another brief show and tell—he shared a new pair of Marc Jacobs rain boots and a designer candle, both discovered at deep discount—inaugurated our first kiss and the budding awareness that we might never speak again.

The chef seemed to have virtually no interest in the details of my life, but by this time I had learned a variety of facts and feelings about his own: his best friend had shot himself in the mouth in high school, he was late to discover girls, his father had married a third cousin, and he planned to open a gourmet popsicle venture called SickPop, with a flagship store in L.A. (outfitted in blonde wood and glass, with the popsicles themselves in individual cellophane wrappers providing the only color) and outposts in Tokyo and Antwerp. I offered, unsolicited, a variety of advice:

1. sweet goat cheese as a key flavor;
2. the embrace of both custards and ices (so that the line contained a spectrum of textures);
3. the absence of chairs at the California store, since popsicles are meant to walk, not sit, with;
4. branding partnership opportunities with ingredient providers;
5. the change-over to soup sales in winter.

I also sternly warned him to anticipate that the plastic wrappers might well frost up, thus dulling the chroma and saturation of his fantasy display.

6. CAMELOT

My mother had a close friend named Dolores—she was an oval social worker with diabetes and a tight bun who wore Marimekko tent dresses and received the absolute highest caliber of catalogs possible. She was obviously on the best mail-order lists, lists that fed and branched off each other, creating a kind of retail tree of life. As far as I knew, all of her non-working hours were spent with the television and the catalogs, and with the foodstuffs she had ordered—pâtés, preserves, dense cake-breads wrapped in foil, and hand-wrought English muffins. My mother sometimes visited her in the evening, returning shortly before my bedtime surrounded by a slightly grouchy cloud of chardonnay, and it was obvious that the conversations accumulating between them contained pieces of both women that existed nowhere else and focused, most likely, on marital dismay.

One Sunday Dolores sat at our kitchen table and spoke of a recent, noteworthy lunch: a well-composed Caesar salad. To conjure it and to give praise to its substantial size, Dolores created a box with her fingers—so that the thumb and forefinger of each hand made C-shapes facing each other, and one was expected to connect the space between the two hands with the dotted line of the imagined salad. Dolores' long, filed nails made the gesture enviable, something only a fully formed woman's hands could pull off, but I was equally distracted by her swollen nail beds. Skin and nail diseases of all kinds—and shortages and excesses in the blood only known via sampling and inspection, clearly visible to some and fully unknowable to others: all of this reliably held my attention. Sinus cavity secrets, bubbles in the blood, subluxations, joint inflammation, ductal trouble, trapped bacteria communities, eustachian tube dysfunction, histamine activity. JFK's constellation of bodily troubles was of great interest to me, as were theories of causality linking his Addison's disease to his sexual addiction and urinary tract infections, bringing his tan and his cortisone shots and his excruciating back pain into one impossible space of unity.

7. COSMETICS

In 2003, I was working on a Dominick Dunne TV documentary when our subject, Max Factor heir, avid surfer, and serial rapist Andrew Luster fled the country in the midst of his trial. He took up residence in Mexico as David Carrera and returned to surfing and margaritas; he found them relaxing. My work revolved around gentle manipulations: convincing his mother to FedEx me all the family photo albums, for instance, and begging the Ventura County DA for Luster's miniDV sex tapes. In the end the bounty hunter Duane "Dog" Chapman captured Luster in Puerto Vallarta. Dog was hoping his achievement would pave the way for his own reality series, but unfortunately bounty hunting is illegal in Mexico and he was arrested.

8. CAVIAR

One evening in the late seventies we received an unexpected visit from Mei Lin Turner, the daughter-in-law of the Scottish anthropologist Victor Turner. Upon taking a seat at the kitchen table, Mei Lin requested caviar and champagne and due to some sort of mutation of probability, we had both on hand. I was already dressed for bed, which granted me the unspoken permission to remain in the kitchen as a benign observer (not a participant), so long as I kept gestures and sounds to a minimum, and I was captivated by the spectacle of my mother and Mei Lin finding intimate communion, mutually affirmed deservedness, under the auspices of miniature orange balls.

Indulge, I ordered them silently.

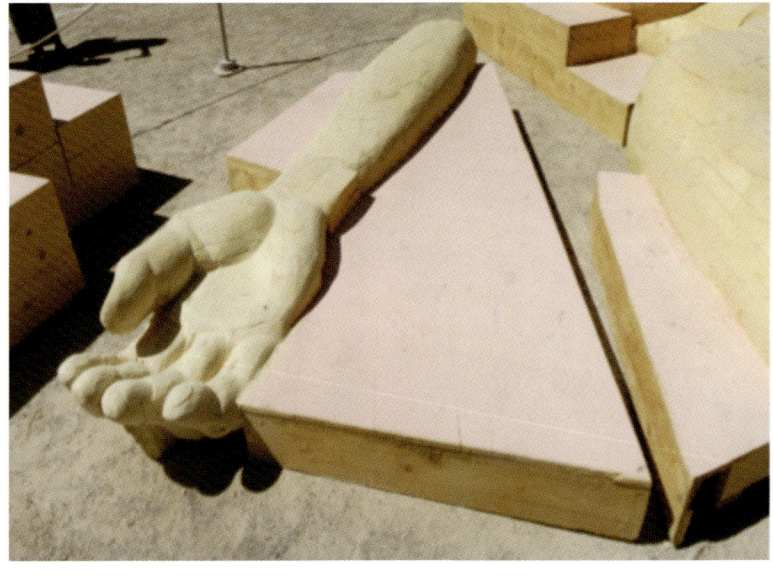

Stage set, *Prometheus Bound*, Epidaurus, Greece.

3.

HEADLINERS & LEGENDS

1.

I called Joan Kennedy to talk about some pictures of her parents that I'd found in a book. She said it was OK if I used them in an episode of *Headliners and Legends with Matt Lauer.*

Maxwell Kennedy is breezy and accessible. He said I could use Robert Kennedy's personal photos of Ethel in casual wear but a few days before the show aired he changed his mind.

Ted Kennedy's former secretary Melody Miller is efficient and friendly. She took a lot of pictures of Ted over the years and now she sells them. I chose one of Joan at the Chappaquiddick funeral with a big bow in her hair.

I became fascinated by Ethel because she had buck teeth and so many kids and still had a nice figure. She'd do anything for Bobby.

The archivist at the JFK Memorial Library is extremely mean. He is in charge of all the pictures but he's not one of the Kennedys; he's a professional.

There's something a little embarrassing about the Kennedy Library. Not the mission but the actual building.

During production, Joan was arrested for drunk driving. We stopped talking.

I flew to Boston to interview Joan's ex-boyfriend. He said he and Joan were like teenagers in love and cooked chicken marsala together at the house in Truro.

At first I was nervous when I was charged with locating a picture of the man Jackie Kennedy had been engaged to before she met JFK, but it wasn't that hard to find. The downside was that the photo came from an old newspaper wedding announcement so it wasn't a high-quality image. The man's face was composed of dots.

Oleg Cassini needed affirmation. He felt that he had been under-recognized in the development of American style.

There was one particular photo of Jackie on crutches in which a cast was wrapped around her leg so precisely that it made a set of perfectly parallel diagonal lines run up her calf. Every time I looked at it I felt like I was being stuck with needles but I was not able to understand why. I did wonder if the photo had been doctored—like when eyelashes are enhanced—but it simply didn't make sense that a cast would warrant that kind of attention.

Once we had assembled all the pieces, Matt Lauer recorded his host wraps. *The Kennedy Women* was complete.

2.

Next I worked on an episode about Goldie Hawn and Kate Hudson.

I called Kate's father Bill Hudson's lawyer and asked him if Bill had any home videos of his daughter as a child. He did and sold them for $7000.

I called Kate's classmate from high school and convinced her to send me an old yearbook. I took the yearbook to a man who makes a decent living panning across still photos with a video camera and shot every picture Kate was in. I got worried that I had lost some of the stray snapshots the girl had stuck inside the yearbook cover but I recovered them all and returned everything with a kind thank you note. I stressed the generosity of the giver.

I flew to Maryland to interview Goldie Hawn's high school drama teacher. One of his sons was living at home at a late age; he had just woken up from a nap and was interested in a snack. It was hard to maintain my interest during the interview and I remember wondering how I had gotten to this point. The cameraman was hitting on me so I thought maybe the rewards and punishments would even out but I later realized that they would not.

I took the crew to Goldie's high school. We stood across the street and zoomed in.

I bought a copy of an old *Playboy* magazine featuring a long interview with a young Goldie. I was pleased that she had been in psychoanalysis, but wondered why it hadn't had more of an impact.

Goldie had been in a couple of long-term relationships before she settled down with Kurt Russell, the love of her life.

The day before we delivered the show to MSNBC, my boyfriend broke up with me. Even though I knew I was lying, I asked him if he thought anyone would ever love me again. He said he didn't feel comfortable predicting the future.

Due to the breakup, I didn't want to go to work the next day but I had to be there at 7 a.m. to receive a special delivery from London of one last master shot of Goldie and her first husband Gus Trikonis getting off a plane at Heathrow Airport. It was wintertime, and they both wore fur.

4.

A VALENTINE FOR MR. WONDERFUL

When Kirk Varnedoe died in the middle of August in 2003, Charlie Rose re-aired an old conversation between them. I took out my video camera and shot Kirk talking for an hour, unsure about why he couldn't simply like Jackson Pollock's paintings without frothing so heavily. Charlie nearly collapsed reviewing Kirk's famous lecturing skills and the two of them smiled in the sweet spiral of knowing art.

That night I dreamt that the best professor in the world taught at the University of Southern Florida. I was willing to go anywhere— even southern Florida—to meet this teacher, so I flew there right away. The teacher was Ed Harris and the cause of his greatness was his invention of an endless glass wall. It was infinite, extending beyond vision in all directions, and when I approached it with him, stood right up against it, I saw ancient Rome on the other side. It was so easy to look at, stretched long and covered in round white building tops.

Four years earlier, at a dinner celebrating Varnedoe's Jackson Pollock retrospective at the Museum of Modern Art, I saw Ed Harris. He was preparing for his Pollock biopic and explaining Helen Frankenthaler's essence to Stephanie Seymour. I was there as the guest of a friend who interned in the Publications Department and had proofread the show catalog four times, and we were seated next to Rosalind Krauss but could not gain any traction, and focused on Brooke Alexander instead. I wore a long carmine silk top over black pants and it was the last night I experienced the rewards of not knowing who I was in such a clean, bubble-like way. I drank so much that I insisted on taking the subway home, and woke up when the D line terminated at Brighton Beach.

Top: Pen and mini paint set, Bangkok, Thailand.
Bottom: Tree at water's edge, Syros, Greece.

5.

FIRSTS & SECONDS

When I first saw Jim Dine's paintings of bathrobes with proud stomachs, I didn't like them. I preferred his hand-colored lithographs of tools.

In Nancy Dine's documentary about her husband, the word "draughtsman" kept coming up, and by the end of the film, it did seem as if Jim were a master draughtsman. He drew as if he were whipping up a milkshake in a fury or starting a tornado.

*

I watched a film about Picasso at work, and I saw that he painted fast, too—in the hopes of making as many choices as possible.

*

I saw the *Torqued Ellipses* twice and then I made a book that read: I SAW THE TORQUED ELLIPSES TWICE ONCE WITH SUGAR ONCE WITH ICE (one word per page).

*

When I was in Paris I saw a man named Edouard four times. The first time we had lunch at Le Palais de Tokyo and then saw a Picabia show. We lost each other on purpose and I slowed down to look at a picture so he would find me. I had something in my eye and I asked him to look. He said he saw a little woman in my eye.

On our final meeting we went to a bookstore to find a French copy of *Goodbye, Columbus*. When we walked out, Edouard said "Bye, baby," as if he were trying out a new American phrase. He kissed me with great noise and motion on both cheeks, as one would a small child. My gift of a small orange and cream-colored F. Picabia book (*Jésus-Christ Rastaquouère*) suddenly seemed wrong, but I gave it to him all the same.

*

I saw Stan Brakhage's *Text of Light* and Jim Davis' *Energies* in one night. In *Text of Light*, close-ups of a sun-hit glass ashtray turned into Hudson River School landscape paintings which turned into Courbet and then Milton Avery. A shudder showed up before each transition, a real hard push that always worked.

*

I ran into my dentist at the theater when I went to see Michel Auder's videos. He sat next to me (with three empty seats between us). Later I went to get my teeth cleaned and he asked, "How was the second movie?" I had run to catch a real French film after I saw him the Auder night. My dentist has a beard that's as short as possible and he makes videos when he's not fixing teeth. His name is Francis.

*

I collapsed on my way to work on Monday and by Tuesday I had fallen in love with my cardiologist, Dr. Rob Silk. His office was decorated with posters from national parks and medals marking athletic achievements under glass. Dr. Silk lifts weights. He has nice hair that's parted on the side and a straight nose.

On Thursday I saw him again. This time he was paler and wore a white polo shirt and a white coat that said CARDIOLOGY in blue letters. The following year I opened the *New York Post* and saw a picture of Dr. Silk. He had been charged with molesting multiple patients and groping a nurse in the elevator.

*

When I had my first show at a gallery, I nearly had a breakdown. One of the owners made me uneasy, and he later lost my negatives.

A few months after the show came down, I brought the owners a gift of two books—one for each of them. I stuck gold stickers with each man's initials on the book meant for him, and I wrote a long thank-you note on an old card covered with jellybeans. Instead of using ribbon, I wrapped a piece of kelly-green paper tape around both books and then pinned the jelly-card on top. It was so pretty, and the gallery was about to close for the summer, so I had to hurry. I made a fast video in the bathroom, explaining why I had prepared the books and my hopes for the future. I made sure to take close-ups of the gift, and I wore pink earrings and an odd blue top with ruffles. My hair happened to be straightened that day, so it seemed like a big occasion.

*

I shouldn't pretend that things only happen where men are concerned and the story of the lost negatives reminds me of the time when a woman with a great big personality and a modest apartment that she made beautiful with paint and artifacts lost a book of drawings that I had made over the course of a year. It was a small white leather book and each drawing was the size of a business card.

*

I once had an art teacher who sat at a desk while the class stood around her and she ran her fingers over pictures of Milton Avery paintings and African masks before we started working.

PART TWO

WRITING ON THE WALL, SCREEN, & SKY

6.

THE HOUR OF THE STAR*

1. Birthday cake, Kikeli Hotel, Ho, Ghana.
2. Bust, Council on Foreign Relations, New York, NY.
* Brazilian writer Clarice Lispector's final novel.

3. European mother and daughter, Tulum, Mexico.
4. Broken Danish chair, Brooklyn, NY.
5. Headstone, B'nai Israel Cemetery, Elizabeth, NJ.

6. Ink spill, *L'Avventura.*
7. Opening title, *Bay of Angels.*
8. Fruit, Shangri-La's Mactan Island Resort, Philippines.

9. Tablecloth, Freedom Hotel, Ho, Ghana.
10. Bedspread light prism, Mt. Vernon, OH.
11. Graduation party, San Juan, Puerto Rico.

7.

THE ART OF TRANSCRIBING A SUNSET

I refuse to be the dupe of a kind of magic which brandishes before an eager public albums of colored photographs instead of the now vanished native masks. Perhaps the public imagines that the charms of the savages can be appropriated through the medium of these photographs.[1]

— Claude Lévi-Strauss

Claude Lévi-Strauss forcefully registers his skepticism about the capacity of color photographs to transmit an anthropological journey in the opening pages of *Tristes Tropiques* (its first sentence: "I hate traveling and explorers"). He wants to keep magic for himself, on the interior of an ethnographic escapade, guarded by the boundaries of his professional expertise and sensitivity; naïve are those who believe native secrets can be imprinted on photographic paper, who fall for identification between color and the real. As he says, "Nowadays, being an explorer is a trade, which consists not, as one might think, in discovering hitherto unknown facts after years of

---

1. Claude Lévi-Strauss, *Tristes Tropiques*, trans. John and Doreen Weightman (New York: Penguin, 1992), 41.

study, but in covering a great many miles and assembling lantern-slides or motion pictures, preferably in color, so as to fill a hall with an audience for several days in succession."[2] The proof-boasting quality of photographic forms, both still and moving, is so obvious that it exposes its own sham. And in his vision of the impressionable who are attracted to such charades and "fill halls," Lévi-Strauss imagines a continuous flow of bodies and misguided curiosities to match the mesmerizing flow of motion pictures: a foil to his solitary excursions and the erratic rhythms of their physical and mental labors. Though he doesn't say so, these colored pictures are clearly a foil to language as well.

But in his "Sunset" chapter—the transcription of a setting sun seen from aboard a Brazil-bound ship, shortly after departing from Marseilles in 1934—Lévi-Strauss rides on color, and produces an optical trip with language. In so doing, he provides my favorite example of the power of color to shock a philosophical investigation into quiet submission, transmission occurring not via the reality-imprint of a photograph but along the surface of a colored picture that's composed of words. Perhaps because he hasn't arrived at his destination yet, some rough, broken-down form of ethnography can only be conducted by documenting a morphology of color; Lévi-Strauss' refusal of the association between the pictorial and the ethnographic quiets down as he gives in to a journey that's narrated by the sky.[3] I read it as a lyric ode to magic without mention of magic by name—not magic-as-ritual, delicately uncovered and

2. Lévi-Strauss, 17–18.

3. The sunset-inspired, voyage-out narratives of anthropologists deserve our attention: ship-board preludes to fieldwork tell us much about the stimulation and imagination of an anthropological mind before the purported objects of study have been reached.

recorded in the heat of an inaccessible jungle, but magic in its most modest, culturally neutral state: as a picture of change.

The vision of a complete performance with so many rapidly dissolving acts, the surprise of finding the gaudy, neon and jewel-toned in the daily, and the drive to narrate the spectacle in detail combine to momentarily topple Lévi-Strauss' professional sense of identification. He no longer needs anthropology; or, anthropology for a moment is contained in the joint beholding and transcription of a sunset: "If I could find a language in which to perpetuate those appearances, at once so unstable and so resistant to description, if it were granted to me to be able to communicate to others the phases and sequences of a unique event which would never recur in the same terms, then…I should in one go have discovered the deepest secrets of my profession."[4] His language in this chapter jumps out of the skin of its usual container; he stretches for the words to mark his vision of the sky and rushes to include it all in eight pages of sunset hypnosis. He sees "bloated but ethereal ramparts, all glistening, like mother of pearl, with pink, mauve and silvered gleams," then a "laminated [mass] like a sheet of metal illuminated from behind, first by a golden, then a vermillion, then a cherry glow"; there are "bulging pyramids and frothy bubblings" and "streaks of dappled blondness decomposing into nonchalant twists" and a "spun glass network of colors…shrimp, salmon, flax, straw" that, with the final setting, becomes "purple, then coal black, and then…no more than an irregular charcoal mark on grainy paper" as night finally arrives.[5] And then he returns to being an anthropologist, making his way through South America without

4. Lévi-Strauss, 62.

5. Lévi-Strauss, 62–69.

the accompaniment of a painted sky. He returns to being a structuralist, a writer, and to black and white.

As evidenced by Lévi-Strauss' professional undoing in its midst, the sunset is a zone of reversal. The day trades places with the night, and announces the turn-over with paint and time; it's a rare site of ocular access to x becoming y in a temporal register that's both fast and slow (fast enough for the entire morphology to unfold in one sitting, slow enough to note and record each transition). When water is part of the tableau, the identities of sea and sky break down too—the shapes of clouds and spills of pink and purple pass back-and-forth. And as the stream of his documentation unfolds, Lévi-Strauss' use of figurative language collects around another kind of reversal: the turning of the sky is linked to forms of art, and the comparative leap that characterizes metaphor finds in the sky the artifacts of culture. "Daybreak is a prelude, the close of day an overture which occurs at the end instead of the beginning, as in old operas." In a double back-and-forth, he notates clouds "immobilized in the form of mouldings representing clouds, but which real clouds resemble when they have the polished surface and bulbous relief of carved and gilded wood." And in the end, the scene is a "photographic plate of night."[6]

Although Lévi-Strauss does not invoke "magic" in his sunset reverie, its presence hovers. For magic in its essence runs on the surprise and gratification of encounters with condensed, sped-up forms of change, foils to the durations by which changes of state—in material form and psychic interiority—take place in non-magical life. Magic offers a display of its own effectivity, turning abstract ideas into objects. In *A General Theory of Magic*, Marcel Mauss tells

---

6. Lévi-Strauss, 62–68.

of a Murring sorcerer, for instance, who produces chunks of quartz from his mouth as proof of a nocturnal encounter with the spirit world.[7] But as Mauss crisscrosses content, geography and time, reviewing demonology, rites and role-acquisition in Australia, Madagascar, and Malaysia at ancient, medieval and contemporary moments, he is most interested in language; he remains a spectator who gets to use logical language and watch its illogical applications at once—the ideal position, perhaps, of the anthropologist. Mauss boils magic down to its core: "The magician knows that his magic is always the same—he is always conscious of the fact that magic is the art of changing." And again: "Between a wish and its fulfillment there is, in magic, no gap...[M]agic's central aim is to produce results."[8] In response to criticism leveled against Mauss for drawing generalizations from such diverse examples, Lévi-Strauss re-framed Mauss' move as the seed of a radical semiotic observation: magic is a turning of the mismatches of language into useful material; it takes the peripheral excess (outside logic, but hovering, waiting for attention) and allows it to motor and fuel the activities of change.[9] As David Pocock explains in his "Foreword" to Mauss' book: "Rituals *do* what words cannot *say*: in *act* black and white can be mixed; the young man is made an adult; spirit and man can be combined or separated at will."[10]

The idea that a photo could not only stand in for a mask, but also carry the mask's contexts, auras and the anthropologist's

7. Marcel Mauss, *A General Theory of Magic*, trans. Robert Brain (New York: Routledge, 2001), 50–51.

8. Mauss, 75–79.

9. David Pocock, "Foreword," *A General Theory of Magic*, 4–8.

10. Pocock, 5.

hard-earned understanding of it, is for Lévi-Strauss an unbearable shortcut. Photography is a variety of magic that he "refuse[s] to be the dupe of." In contrast, in his beholding and written tracking of the sunset, Lévi-Strauss finds a way to stay with the stream of his consciousness without break—the sunset holds his perception and reverie, contains and is coextensive with it: the sunset functions doubly, as any satisfying magical event does, as object and stream.

*

An overwhelming number of videos made by the French-born American artist Michel Auder (b. 1944) feature sunsets: *Brooding Angels* (1988), *Personal Narrative of Travels to Bolivia* (1995), *Polaroid Cocaine* (1993), *Rooftops and Other Scenes* (1996), *TV America* (1988), *Voyage to the Center of the Phone Lines* (1993), and others. A sunset and a videotape are somehow meant to commune: the furriness of the tableau of a dropping sun; the temporariness; the bleeding colors, pale and fluorescent at once, tending toward gradation and chiaroscuro; and the strange impossibility of their location in the sky—all find ideal recognition among televisual tubes and scan lines and their chromatic tendencies. Video is prone to disappointment in a variety of directions. It degrades with ease, can produce unsolicited clarity, stubbornly refusing mystery, and it fails to behave and gratify like film. But when it finds its proper objects and gestures under the auspices of the right light, a poem is made. Auder once told me that making videos feels like working with language: like writing.

In *Voyage to the Center of the Phone Lines*, Auder holds dissociated and urgent time side-by-side for 55 minutes. He has gathered, selected and ordered fragments of intercepted phone conversations (he obsessively scanned mobile calls between 1987 and 1989) for his audio track and placed them on top of slowly alternating, gazed-out-at images from a quiet beach retreat. Many images frame some combination of sea, sky and horizon line—often fringed by the silhouettes of tree tips and leaf edges—at alternating moments of daytime and sunset, noontime azure expanses and evening tableaux of the sinking sun existing side-by-side. The shots are devoid of human figures, and there's a suggestion that the pictures were generated out of solitude, perhaps spurred on by notes of engaged malaise. Rain falls on bricks; seagulls fly across the water; beads of water rest on pine-needle tips; a daytime moon hangs in the sky. Auder is not lost in the wilderness, however: in the second half of the video we encounter a beach house interior with a fireplace, car racing on TV, and windows through which to continue to watch the sky.

The pairs of voices from the phone calls are common and raw—the content is not always alarming but the sameness that binds them is: these conversations are marked by intimate and incisive stabs at the truth, and many of them by pressing concerns about sexuality and sanity. Lovers anticipate sex and taunt each other with guesses about who loves the other more; parents fret over their teenage daughter's tendency toward unprotected sex with an unsavory boy and fantasize about forms of violent punishment; two female friends make distinctions among kinds of sex with types of men; two men wonder how to re-engage an emotionally withdrawing girlfriend; a woman describes feeling acutely rejected by a boyfriend who's not keen on sex; two friends criticize a third for cutting off all contact with her mother and calling it bravery. There are questions about masturbation and molestation and therapy and the ethics of skipping a birthday party, and about how to best praise God and gain membership to his kingdom.

It's not enough, though, to call Michel Auder a "voyeur"—the term most often used to explain what's undeniably and uncannily fascinating about his work. The tag of "voyeur" stems logically from the artist's tendency to capture images from angles of silent, secret or furtive observation, as well as from the fact that his biography and body of work are full of well-inscribed proper names—Viva, Cindy Sherman, Alice Neel, to name a few—and hence many of his videos offer the viewer a kind of ethnographic access to some of the many art-worlds in which Auder has worked and lived. But this tag is of little use in the effort to fully encounter and articulate the poetics and rhetorical acrobatics of Auder's work, which spans four decades and many hundreds of tapes.

Yes, Auder is certainly listening in in *Voyage*—but his voyeurism goes way beyond the perversely motivated acts of observation that we associate with the term. I see Auder-as-voyeur collecting in order to confirm a suspicion, intervening in the streams of talk that contain everything we might ever want to know. It requires great labor to collect the scripts of one's own thought, and even more to collect those of strangers and reformulate them into an object of some kind—a video.

I can't watch *Voyage to the Center of the Phone Lines* without thinking of William James' "Stream of Thought" essay from his 1890 *Principles of Psychology*: a proposal that thought is not made of starts and stops and discrete ideas but is instead continuous, interruption-free, and ever-changing ("we never descend twice into the same stream"). The sole place James does assert a gap—"the greatest breach in nature"—is between individual minds:

> The only states of consciousness that we naturally deal with are found in personal consciousnesses, minds, selves, concrete particular I's and you's. Each of these minds keeps its own

thoughts to itself. There is no giving or bartering between them. No thought even comes into direct sight of a thought in another personal consciousness than its own. Absolute insulation, irreducible pluralism, is the law.[11]

The implicit charge is that this breach is so profound that we misperceive it in every place but the one where it actually exists—we treat it as occurring between and among thoughts and days and objects, and we value associated gestures of articulation, enunciation and concision. James doesn't ask us to banish the recognition of separate objects and moments of thought, but simply to view them in the context both of the "greatest breach" between minds and of the ceaseless stream within a single one. In *Voyage*, like so many of Auder's videos, there is both bleeding—between day and night, water and sky, and among the private pains of strangers—and the satisfying static of switching channels as we leave the stream of one conversation and enter the current of another.

*

Shots of sunsets in *Voyage* punctuate the video with a kind of focus and straightforward shock that mimic the urgency of these lovers and relatives and friends. Each finds the setting sun in a pose of distinct gesture and coloration (it is unclear if the images come from a single night or were collected from many). The water is black; a neon pink halo surrounds the sun; the sky is striped by yellow and green strokes;

11. William James, "Stream of Thought," *Principles of Psychology* (Cambridge: Harvard UP, 1981), 221.

the setting sun shrinks in a turquoise sky over navy water; lavender, fuchsia and peach gradations float above a dark purple sea. Each shot is startling for its difference from the others, and for the spectrum of coloration that's so unlike the pared-down palettes of the daytime shots. The night tells secrets. The speakers tell secrets too—not so much to each other as to us—because they are neither meant for us nor for assembly alongside those of the other callers.

The secret is both that we're all having versions of the same conversations and that culture provides few ways for us to know and encounter this fact. The secret is that we need transcripts from the stream of thought and from the flow of talk for our own experiences of health and communion. Sexuality is insistent and confused. Women speak of the workings of desire with certainty among themselves—and invoke knowing these things less surely with a male lover. We've heard of these dilemmas before, but we don't know them in this form, all at once and from the mouths of strangers.

*

Woman: People who are not God's children are going to be blinded.

Man: But it's also up to us to bring as many into the flock as we can. We have to listen to people. I pray that he gives me time to do that…

Woman: God is good—he answers prayers, but we have to really keep in touch with him; it's a two-way street.

Man: I read the Bible every day. I speak the Word every single day when I do have time. That's kinda hard sometimes.

Woman: God doesn't expect more than what you can do—he knows, but you can lift your thoughts up to him. Just your thoughts.

Man: I try to be still before the Lord and I try to tune into what he has to say…

Woman 1: I don't want it to be like we're gonna get together and go to bed…

Woman 2: You know what happens, when you have so little time together, that's what ends up happening.

Woman 1: And I don't like that. I want there to be some substance…quite frankly to me, that's kind of boring…

Woman 2: When I was going out with Russell, I felt like I was fucking dessert at the end of every night…

Woman 1: I'm trying to learn you shouldn't be insulted by that, but it's like, I don't want to be this object that gets fucked…. It's like, hello? I'd rather just cuddle up with a guy…

Woman 2: Oh, I love to cuddle. For me that's even better.

Woman 1: Oh yeah, I love that…

Woman 2: I just like guys that make me melt. Oh, God.

Woman 1: [X] made me very responsive to him because he was very caressing, and he wasn't rough. It was like he cared about your body.

Daughter: Mama wants to know if it's convenient for you to talk to him?

Father: Talk to *her*?

Daughter: Yeah. Alright 'cause there's something she's gotta tell you…

Father: Is it about you?

Daughter: Yeah.

Father: What is it now?

Daughter: You're gonna be disappointed but it's something.

Father: Don't tell me you saw Billy again.

[…]

Father: I think there's something radically wrong with her.

Mother: You don't know the worst of it. She's been sleeping with him. She slept with him last night.

Father: What do you mean she slept with him last night?

Mother: She's not been using protection and mind you he's been sleeping with every Tom, Dick and Harry.

[…]

Mother: I think you need to keep a tighter rein on her, Jack…

Father: I'm gonna beat the shit out of her if she lied to me. I'm just forewarning you. I don't give a fuck how old she is. She's gonna feel the back of my hand.

Mother: Don't hit her on the face.

**

Woman: Think about this—my father supposedly according to Uncle Morgan was sexually abused more than anyone else.

Man: That's what I understand as well.

Woman: What if my father did it to Garth and we don't know?

Man: That somehow would not surprise me.

Woman: How do we find out?

[...]

Woman: How about masturbation?

Man: Masturbation is a big question. Lots of kids masturbate.

Woman: I know that, Philip, but they don't do it in the TV room on 8th Avenue in front of Pat and my mother at 3 years old…

Man: Something is very, very, very wrong.

In *Voyage*, Auder offers us rare samples from the chaos of spoken language. The video seems like a direct response to the question Wallace Stevens poses in the first stanza of "A Fading of the Sun":

Who can think of the sun costuming clouds
When all people are shaken
Or of night endazzled, proud,
When people awaken
And cry and cry for help?[12]

All images from Michel Auder's *Voyage to the Center of the Phone Lines*.

12. Wallace Stevens, "A Fading of the Sun," in Frank Kermode and Joan Richardson, eds., *Wallace Stevens: Collected Poetry and Prose* (New York: Library Classics of the United States, Inc., 1997), 112–113.

8.

THE SPLATTER TECHNIQUE

An Interior Monologue Between the Narrator and Carolee Schneemann

1.

When you introduced *Hart of London*, the Jack Chambers film, at Light Industry in Brooklyn, you said Chambers was a painter before he was a filmmaker.

He used aluminum spray paint straight from the can. You had to walk by to see the pieces completely: the image was dependent on light. He made *Hart of London* in the shadow of his own death. He was diagnosed with leukemia in 1968 and died 10 years later.

Did he fall in love after the diagnosis?

No. His mother was dying of cancer in 1961 and he moved back to London from Madrid to be with her. So by the time he got sick he had already learned to acclimate to cancer. It wasn't like some invigorating shock.

I like the idea of the kind of man who would marry within a year of his mother's death, with his sadness still at least semi-intact. The simplicity of the switchover from one love object to another is

Top: Photographs of glass tumblers, Chicago, IL.
Bottom: Napkin ring from the wedding of Sigmund Freud and Martha Bernays, Vienna, Austria.

touching—as if it indicates a kind of great sensitivity on his part. In my mind his lips darken and his eyelashes lengthen permanently, remaining forever just a touch moist from proximity to tears.

Grief works wonders for sexuality. But funeral sex is generally a woman's domain—if she can find someone she doesn't quite love but trusts—someone she can make demands on since all bets are off. It's a rare chance to grieve, dissociate and achieve orgasm at once.

I was taken by how soft you seemed the *Hart of London* night—you didn't appear to be terribly stimulated by the sound of your own voice even with a microphone nearby, and yet you were open. And there was a man in the audience—a kind of middle-aged Jewish guy in fleece who seemed reliable. I assumed he was your boyfriend. I got the sense neither of you was over-extending yourself to acquire an identity.

I've had time. Sometimes you do need a man to provide a good dose of narcissism so you can dilute it in a bucket of lukewarm water: like a quarter teaspoonful of cranberry concentrate or indigo dye. It can be very effective for revving up desire. The challenge, of course, is to integrate that colored water into a loving, trustworthy relationship. You might be able to get your hands on the bucket, but you rarely get around to watering the garden.

Is that how it is with the Jewish guy?

God, no. Later you'll get to dropping out, down under desire—where it smooths out and the other person is jelly somehow—not jam, but jelly—you know, he holds his form, but you can still see his plainest self, below the radar. The cutting edge of gender softens, but not so much that it ruins the experience—it's a non-requirement of the knife's edge.

Like those tall seven-layer cakes from New Jersey bakeries—that sensation of the vague border between layers as you cut down. Sometimes it's even a two-handed endeavor in terms of guiding the knife. It's a slide but there's friction, and these cakes are expensive, too. They stay together under the outside shell. I've never understood women who like the overripe peach—some guy who will just split in two and the pit will come tumbling out.

It's difficult to see others glide along on the gentle waves of love when you have to pause to make carvings into surfaces every few minutes.

But you made drawings on your father's prescription pills.

A fine-tipped pen on an uncoated tablet is fantastic—you can hear each stroke. You think you're in so much control and a minute later the ink has bled into a giant spider web. If you don't want a mess you can use a mechanical pencil.

My dad once sensed that I might have a talent for illustration and asked me to copy a cereal box cartoon at breakfast. I didn't do a good job. One night we discovered that my brother could speak backwards when he was going to bed and called me "Hakeber" and my mom, whose name is Jane, "Enaj." We tested to see if he could say some other words—first "Pluto" and then "anti-disestablishmentarianism"—backwards, and he could.

You're worried that you're a masochist. Just ignore it until it goes away. That's what happens in the onward march of female hetero-sexuality—one day you'll wake up and the tension will be unsustainable. It will cease playing itself out in the theater of public histrionics and will go lie quietly in some kind of internal jewelry box, with velvet-lined drawers. Ideally at the end there's grace and the phallus is as much yours as it is his. It's a process that's much too slow and unsightly for women to tell each other about—that's why we're always re-inventing the wheel.

Each one has to deplete her own resources for herself. Plus, can you imagine telling your daughter about this ahead of time? It would be like moving to Poland for good.

Copying the Old Masters, Kunsthistorisches Museum, Vienna, Austria.

2.

Everyone wants to know who dripped first.

This surprises you?

But you did a lot of smearing—and the *Interior Scroll* may have dripped.

Listen. It didn't. Roger Vadim invented Brigitte Bardot who invented the New Wave.

The night after the *Hart of London* screening I dreamt that you taught a class on how to make a drip painting. The space was open, industrial and a long horizontal strip of raw canvas hung from the ceiling by hooks. Like a hand-made but perfectly functioning machine, buckets of paint just above the canvas poured out their contents in order from left to right, creating huge vertical spills—a sequence of colors in fast succession. The film programmer Mark McElhatten ran down the length of the canvas in time with the pouring; he pulled each spill of paint down to the bottom edge of the canvas, and had to function in perfect sync with the whole mechanism. In the end it looks like a Morris Louis painting and it's laid out on the ground. I chose a raw spot on the canvas—a place untouched by paint—and sat there. You said there should be no areas of canvas showing. But didn't Morris Louis leave areas of raw canvas? I asked. Morris Louis was not an important painter, you replied. "I invented this method." I couldn't believe that you had set this elaborate thing up just to teach us something. It was so thought-through, massive and delicate

Top: Strangers, Lucerne, Switzerland.
Bottom: Display of men's shirts, Warsaw, Poland.

at once. I wanted to know if this was just a demo or a real painting. It turned out it was art and you were going to hang it in your retrospective.

We usually see the mark of the painter afterwards—we're so pleased when a painting's still got mountain ridges in it with a dried gloss on top—remnants of the process. But seeing the paintbrush distribute the paint is something else. And even in the Clouzot film about Picasso the main show is the battle between the camera and the brush. To keep the brushwork-in-process dilated is something else. Morris never did that. But he died the same year he was diagnosed with lung cancer, so he didn't have a lot of time to push himself further.

Did Ruth Kligman?

Did she push herself? No. Ruth remained vain but became more generous as she aged. She liked to recall the time Franz Kline confided in her about the pain of painting. "They think it's easy. They don't know it's like jumping off a 12-story building every day."

9.

THE INCUBATORS

SPECTACLE ON A GREEN LAWN

The sun went down in June of 2008, and Robert Beavers offered spare guidance to the 200 pilgrims who had gathered in the remote mountains of Arcadia in the Peloponnese to watch Orders III–V of the American filmmaker Gregory Markopoulos' 80-hour *Eniaios*. Beavers, organizer of the three-night screening event called the Temenos, also a filmmaker, and Markopoulos' long-time partner, invoked the Greek god of healing Asclepios. Ailing visitors seeking a cure slept inside the god's sanctuary in a state of *enkoimesis*, or incubation. The next morning, a priest interpreted the resulting dreams and found in them the counsel of the god. Cured visitors thanked Asclepios by tossing gold into a fountain or returning later bearing altars, statues and replicas of once-afflicted organs. Markopoulos (1928–1992) conceived of the spacing among the flickering images in *Eniaios* in the hopes of nurturing Asclepian incubation in his spectators.[1]

---

1. He "imagine[d] himself a member of an emergent, select order of psychic healers…possessing the skill to subliminally plumb the pre-verbal mysteries of an archaic past," wrote Kirk Winslow. "Intergalactic Trance-Migration," *Millennium Film Journal* 32/33 (Fall 1998): 79–80.

Six months earlier, Beavers had presented his own *Pitcher of Colored Light* (2007) and a reel from *Eniaios* at the Views from the Avant-Garde program of the New York Film Festival—my first encounter with the work of both artists—and the impressions left on me were so distinct that I had found my way to Greece with little rationale beyond the beckoning force of those images. I knew almost nothing about Markopoulos' films, and Beavers' brief mention of Asclepios on the opening Temenos evening offered a welcome structure with which to contain the stimulations of the coming days. I reached back to a dream from the night before, my first in Greece, and saw that incubation had begun.

I had dreamt of an egg-shaped man, a New Yorker, TV producer, and hustler, whose seductions I could only partially resist. He had the oversized and suited body of Wallace Stevens, and a neverending apartment of jewel-colored rooms. My feelings about this man were mixed: the old-fashioned aura of showbiz around him struck me as corrupt, but time alone in his apartment led me to gather the possibility of his depths. I learned that he had spent time in Paris as a young man—in snapshots he was tan and thin, dashing in a white uniform. And after a nap and a face-washing (all my makeup went down the drain), I met him uptown at a semicircular leather booth for brandy. In the final moments of the dream, he created a wild spectacle in the middle of a green park lawn.

He had assembled a bouquet of golf clubs, and attached to the top of each a spray of colored feathers, mimicking a blossom. At the last minute a woman searched for a dark blue feather—the tableau of colors was not correctly balanced, and the addition of blue to one corner of the bouquet-top fixed the composition. And then a handful of children helped send the bouquet into the air; it grew bigger according to my lifted vantage point in the sky. The egg-shaped man was a spectacle-maker. He had launched the feather-flowers for the pleasure of the children.

Like an analysand's first dream, this one was a collage of pre-figuration: the picture of a color spectacle in the sky over a lawn (the Temenos screening situation itself); the idea of cleansing and purification rituals (the face-washing, nap and brandy) necessary, according to the conventions of Asclepian mythology, to prepare for the incubatory dream-state; a deep ambivalence about submitting to a masterful figure whose visionary powers, creative bravura, and maleness are inextricably bound; and a wish for involvement in the creative act (the woman's blue feather addition) beyond the position of worshipful spectatorship.

THE FACILITATING FRAME

As Order III wound through the projector, local children arrived at the grassy clearing prepared by volunteers earlier that week, mowed and strewn with red bean bags. The children sat close to the screen (stored with a local carpenter since the 2004 Temenos event, and then reassembled, painted and tethered to the ground), and erupted into spastic laughter at the sight of red- and blue-suited art pair Gilbert and George, featured just before a series of portraits of artists and patrons—painter David Hockney, art historian Daniel-Henry Kahnweiler, surrealist Leonor Fini, dealer Hans Schlegel, ballerina Marcia Haydée, sculptor Barbara Hepworth, Zurich café proprietress Hulda Zumsteg and poet Edouard Roditi—in Markopoulos' "Genius" and "European Portraits" reels. The laughter followed the flashing pattern of the images: frame-long glimpses of Gilbert and George (two lips divided by a seam; a hand in a pocket; a shiny button on matte fabric; a point of black hair resting over a white arc of collar) catalyzed eruptions that bloomed and died down in rhythm with the silent screen. Like these, many *Eniaios* images are only one frame (1/24th of a second) long, and all are bracketed and isolated from each other by intervening lengths of black and clear leader. The unit of the single frame and the still image were preoccupying, essential elements of cinema for Markopoulos: "It is, perhaps, a fallacy to believe that film is constant movement."[2]

A central figure in the American avant-garde in the 1950s and 60s (in addition to filmmaking, he published extensively in Jonas Mekas' *Film Culture*), Markopoulos grew discontent with American screening and distribution conditions, and he and Beavers left the U.S. for Europe in 1967. He had wanted to live in Europe since his first visits to Greece and Italy in the 1950s, and the two spent the next several decades there in self-imposed exile. Markopoulos refused screenings, removing his films from distribution and demanding the excision of a chapter about his work from P. Adams Sitney's *Visionary Film*.[3] In 1980 organizers cancelled a screening of *The Illiac Passion* (his 1967 interpretation of *Prometheus Bound* starring Andy Warhol and Jack Smith) at the National Gallery in Athens when they learned of the film's substantial nudity. Another screening in Tripoli similarly fell apart. So Markopoulos walked out of Lyssaraia, his Arcadian ancestral village, and found the spot where his films were meant to be seen. "We chose a site surrounded by terraced fields, suspended in a sparkling

---

2. Gregory Markopoulos, "The Intuition Space," *Millennium Film Journal* 32/33 (Fall 1998): 72.

3. It was re-incorporated into the 2002 edition.

atmosphere with a view that reaches to Olympia and the Ionian coast," Beavers recalled.[4]

Markopoulos had written about his idea for the Temenos during the 1970s (*temenos* is an ancient Greek word meaning "a piece of land set apart for the worship of a god" or "sacred grove"); it was to function as an open-air theater as well as an archive and library for his and Beavers' work. Discovery of the site freed him to conceive of his monumental final film, the silent, 16mm *Eniaios* (meaning "unity" and "uniqueness"). Made of re-edited footage from all his previous films and meant to supercede them as an integrated epic work, *Eniaios* contains 100 individual titles in 22 cycles, or orders, of three to five hours each. Markopoulos spent the final decade of his life working on the project, created exclusively for the Temenos site; it was fully edited and notated when he died in 1992, but not yet printed. He felt he had seen *Eniaios* by winding through its 170 reels.

In 1980, a handful of foreign guests and dozens of visitors from the region, including six priests and their families, attended the first open-air Temenos screening—a "symbolic effort in [the] direction" of Markopoulos' ultimate vision. There was neither running water nor public buses; the "only existing road was one that could make you fear for your life, or at least for the life of your car," Beavers said.[5] Early September screenings continued annually until 1987 (when Beavers and Markopoulos turned their attentions to archiving and preservation), followed by the *Eniaios* premiere (Orders I and II) in 2004 and the second and third *Eniaios* screenings in 2008 and 2012.

---

4. Tony Pipolo, "An Interview with Robert Beavers," *Millennium Film Journal* 32/33 (Fall 1998): 31.

5. Pipolo, 27, 31.

The tiny town of Loutra, where Temenos pilgrims stayed,
is known for its therapeutic springs. According to Asclepian
mythology, purification rituals prepare cure-seekers for the
incubatory dream-state.

Temenos 2008:
He had launched the flowers for the pleasure of
the children.

On the night of our arrival, townspeople welcomed us in Lyssaraia with grilled meat, bow-shaped cookies and local wine. Diagonal sunrays shot out of a gathering of peach-tipped clouds like a Divine Mercy painting, and the sky was so low and at ease among the rows of receding mountains that the sunset appeared to rise out of the ground. The birthplace of Markopoulos' father, who emigrated to Toledo, Ohio, where Markopoulos was born (but spoke only Greek until age six), Lyssaraia has a winter population of 10, including one child and one woman.

DIALOGUE IN BLACK AND WHITE

Each evening, two buses brought 150 Temenos pilgrims from Loutra (a tiny spa village known for its therapeutic natural springs where most of the foreign guests stayed) 20 km north to a mountaintop spot just outside Lyssaraia. We walked another kilometer on sweet-smelling, winding *monopati* down to the screening site as the sun shifted and set.

When projection began, the sky was dark but a handful of clouds still alert; later the sky blackened and stars replaced the clouds. Everything decomposed into a series of steps: in the die-down of an image a few frames long (followed immediately by black leader), I counted eight stages before my eyes registered true black. The falling of night, that fact that ushered in the start-up of projection, revealed its own stages under the auspices of the screen. And from the bus window I counted eight layers of mountains: they looked like paper cut-outs.

In the transition from clear leader to black, the border of the screen disappeared and a flame chased after the receding light; then the screen reconstituted itself, matching the tone and hue of the sky. At times, following a spell of white light, the screen undulated, coronated with a neon halo. And the screen was liable to slide as well; its transparent, superimposed twin accompanied my eyes into fully black regions of the sky. But *Eniaios* is also literally embedded with a black and white dialogue: Markopoulos encoded titles into the film by giving each of the 24 letters of the Greek alphabet a numerical measure, translatable into a corresponding number of frames of leader (alpha is one frame, beta is two, etc.). The title letters alternate in color: the first is clear, the second black.

Eniaios offers a kind of primal-scene access, usually denied, to the dynamics between the screen itself and the image contained within it. The separation between images makes possible glimpses of perceptual overlap and bleeding free from their prescribed presence in the form of cross-dissolves and superimpositions; instead the eyes, screen and sky conspire to create these effects.[6]

Walking to the site on the second evening, I stared at the setting sun for too long, and a constellation of dots with uneven, cartoonish edges flew before my eyes. It looked just like a film I had seen before: *Scherzo* (1939) by Norman McLaren. I recalled suddenly that I had seen the word *scherzo* written on the side of a purple and yellow polka-dot box in the window of a closed shop in Megalopolis earlier that day. The box and word had been deposited, but disappeared until the sunspots retrieved them along with McLaren's tiny film.

---

6. The few superimpositions in *Eniaios* come from in-camera editing.

On the precipice of the first four-hour screening, Beavers had given us permission to fall asleep. Let the mind wander, he said. Do not worry about retaining the images. Brief spells of cinematic snoring had never been so acceptable—simply part of the Temenos landscape. One evening, I sat next to a woman who snored for three hours. When the last reel ended, she promptly awoke and turned to me: "There were a lot fewer people snoring tonight, weren't there?"

But I was hesitant to believe Beavers. I kept running lists of fleeting *Eniaios* images, attempts to fix them into permanence alternating with self-instructions to release control and observations about the impulse to bring language into the process of image-intake: *Woman in blue seated in blue chair, with something on her lap that's black and white—Stop naming the image, identifying it!—NAVY is all I will say—Bald head turns, radical black stripe of eyeglasses across side of head—Woman seated under Chagall in gold frame, pink tulips with white rims on table—Forced to engage with a perceptual unit that's not the unit of the edited piece of film—Jewels: the window portals, the short images—Big Dipper just dropped!— Relationship b-w revelation of the single image and coming into being of the entire film—Amoeba angel fresco? swaddled in lots of clear leader, vv short.*

Daytime conversations circled around comparisons of night-time attention: Did you close your eyes? Fall asleep? Look at the stars? On the first evening, a British book indexer explained wild almond tree grafting (hybridizes well with peaches and apricots) and olive tree terracing to me as we drove to the screening site. Afterwards he looked profoundly depleted. "Are you disappointed?"

I asked. "No," he said. "But it was arduous." Beavers acknowledged "questioning where the border is between intensity and exhaustion"; we all shared a sense of the labor of the viewing experience, though it led some to crumple (and to locate the problem in themselves— as a failure of taste, vision, or understanding) and electrified others. Beavers was delighted in the attention he'd witnessed over the last two days, he said on the third, but disappointed by the distracted bootleggers, who added, without permission, an array of glowing LCD screens to the starry screening site.

Legends of Markopoulos—his ego, mastery, and gigantic vision—floated, vaguely threatening, over Loutra. When Beavers expressed polite disapproval of the stealth recording, a fantasy of boiling Markopoulos (he would have grabbed the cameras and thrown them on the ground!) developed as a comparative foil. When Beavers returned to the screening site three times on one evening, to pick up straggling walkers and recover the briefcase and passport he'd left behind, someone suggested Markopoulos continued to control the Temenos site from above, keeping Beavers there.

In the end I found the anticipated specter of Markopoulos' ego flimsy and irrelevant. He had created a spectacle so thoroughly committed to ephemerality and subjective vision that I felt perfectly safe receiving what Beavers called the "gift" of the Temenos without contingent pressure to worship a new god. I never sensed that Markopoulos, like the Asclepian priests, instructed his pilgrims on the proper thank you gift (*iatra*) for a cure. Instead, all signs pointed *away* from the object—the thing represented in the film image, the artist himself, as well as his intention—and toward an encouragement to *use* the Temenos as freely and particularly as one could. An encounter with *Eniaios* is one with a lifetime of vision, spanning the five decades of Markopoulos' film career and spread across two lives (since Markopoulos' death, Beavers has thoroughly dedicated himself to manifesting the Temenos). Contact with, and personal acclimation to, such long swaths of vision-in-formation is one of the primary Temenos gifts, and perhaps following one's own use of its equally lengthy aftermath is one kind of reciprocity.[7] But there is no rush to announce results.

I dreamt of a female artist, one with meager talents, preparing to make Christmas gifts. Soon she would order small circular pieces of wood: charms. In her world there is an appreciation for any form of creative output, even if the result is not art.

VIEWS FROM EPIDAURUS

Stories of sickness and cure floated around Loutra too. Slightly disoriented and far from home, bound by the shared journey, strangers-turning-to-friends traded intimate tales with ease: the survival of two heart attacks and a wildly incompetent doctor; the rapid decline of a close friend from metastasized cancer—no time for closure; the physically ill or emotionally limited spouse who did not come along on the Temenos trip; the discovery of therapy in the midst of a dusty marriage; the patient (this told by a therapist) who rejected every love object to avoid potential loss. P. Adams Sitney told a story of Maya Deren's response to fellow

---

7. Per Lewis Hyde in *The Gift: Imagination and the Erotic Life of Property*, the livelihood of a gift is dependent on its ongoing circulation—it can't be hoarded, set aside, protected, or stopped, but must be continually folded back into movement. The medium of cinema, then, has great gift-giving potential; in the case of *Eniaios*, the flash-like encoding of imagery into spectators' minds facilitates one untraceable variety of gift-passage.

filmmaker Stan VanDerBeek's announcement that he had cancer. I'm so sorry, Deren said. I put a curse on you because you didn't wear a suit to my screening. She reversed the curse in a voodoo ceremony with spilled blood—and VanDerBeek went into remission for the next 15 years.

Like Markopoulos' screening site, the Asclepian sanctuary in the coastal town of Epidaurus was called a *temenos*. It was here that the sterile, paralyzed, broken and blind came, looking for a miracle. The Epidaurians believed Asclepios was born on the summit of Mt. Titthion (Greek for "nipple"), a mountain famous for its medicinal plants that graduated into the tranquil plains of his sanctuary—today a wide field of ruins and an archaeological museum featuring shards and reproductions of the thank-you statuaries left for the god.

Suffering pilgrims followed a series of preparatory steps prior to the climax of curative incubation: a walk along the Sacred Way, supplication at the feet of a statue of the god, purification at a fountain, sacrificial offering (an ox from the rich, fruit from the poor), and submission to priests and singers who chanted hymns in order to open the soul to a visit from the god.

Narratives of Asclepian miracles were recorded on stone tablets; over 70 have survived:

Pandaros the Thessalian had blemishes on his forehead. Whilst sleeping in the Abato [incubation room] he had a vision. The god wound a band around his brow. He ordered him to come out of the Abato, to remove the band and dedicate it to the temple. At daybreak he arose from his bed and removed the band. His forehead was completely clear. The blemishes were stuck to the band. Then he offered it to the temple.

A certain woman from Messene, called Nikoboule, longed to have a child. She slept in the Abato and the god appeared in her dream holding a large snake. The snake slept with her. Inside a year the woman gave birth to two sons.[8]

Two days after the conclusion of the Temenos screenings, I arrived in Epidaurus. I was looking for the very first image in the *Eniaios* "Dedication" reel, a close-up of the ruin-stones at the Pyre of Heracles resting on emerald green grass, but the grass under the Asclepian sanctuary fragments was parched and tan. A bus arrived in the parking lot, and I sat by an elderly priest. He studied a blue plastic bag and then folded it carefully into a single compact square, and spent the rest of the ride sneering at a young girl in white short-shorts who talked unselfconsciously on her phone behind us. "Po, po, po," he shook an irritable finger at her.

I returned to Nafplion, the harbor town with marble streets I had chosen for its proximity to the Asclepian ruins, for a final night. After the Temenos weekend, Nafplion was barely tolerable, designed for tourists looking for encounters with new varieties of tchotchkes—whimsical neon daisies with smiling faces, Victorian marionettes, and marbleized candles shaped like gods. I fell asleep to the flickers of an unfamiliar Mark Wahlberg movie, broken to pieces by a repeating Bacardi ad.

That night I dreamt that I approached the two organizers of Views from the Avant-Garde (where less than a year ago I had first

8. Angeliki Charitonidou, *Epidaurus: The Sanctuary of Asclepios and the Museum* (Athens, Clio Editions: 1978), 14.

encountered Markopoulos' and Beavers' work) as they stood at a circular table. I suggested that next year's program cover boldly feature the acronym made from the event's initials: "VAG." They looked at me blankly, and I slapped them simultaneously on their backs, attempting to diffuse the tension and condescend all at once. "Alright then, we'll find a good picture of a robot and use that instead!" I said firmly and walked away.[9]

WRITING ON THE WALL

It was Ezra Pound, her former fiancé, who suggested to the Imagist poet and prose writer H.D. (Hilda Doolittle, 1886–1961) that the fused serpent-thistle picture mysteriously embossed on her imagination had Asclepian roots. Symbol of death and healing, a snake often accompanies the god in ancient images, twisted around his staff. H.D.'s private image—a coiled serpent and a thistle carved into two halves of a stone block—came to her in a dream, or "merely a flash of vision" (she wasn't sure which).[10] Born into a Moravian community in Bethlehem, Pennsylvania, H.D. probed the mystical sources and circulations of her creative powers in *The Gift* (written 1941–43), and spent a lifetime de-coding and transmitting personal symbols and signposts in poems, memoirs and novels. Pound first suggested "H.D." as a moniker, and it stuck; Doolittle said it provided a useful out from the pun of her last name.

---

9. Filmmaker Su Friedrich may have had something similar in mind; after the announcement of the 2008 *Views* program, she wrote to the organizers chastising them for their ongoing failure to curate the work of more women. Her letter was widely circulated by email.

10. H.D., *Tribute to Freud* (New York: New Directions, 1974), 64.

H.D. and Markopoulos were entwined in my mind, a picture sealed by their joint allegiance to Asclepios. Like Markopoulos, H.D. was an encoder; she fantasized about brains-as-telegraphs: "We want receiving centers for dots and dashes."[11] Both American experimenters who spent much of their lives in Europe, the two are bound by a primal identification with Greece as an originary creative source (H.D.'s entire corpus engages ancient mythology and literature); concerns with incubation, sleep and cure; and devotion to film (H.D. wrote regularly for the journal *Close Up* and participated in the experimental filmmaking group POOL in the 1920s and 30s).

When Beavers told me that Stan Brakhage once gave Markopoulos H.D.'s *Helen in Egypt* as a gift, my desire to find her, to set the two artists side-by-side, hardened into a necessity. I liked the idea of metabolizing the Temenos under the feminine guidance of Doolittle. And it was just a day's trip from Nafplion, in her room at the Grand Hotel D'Angleterre et Belle Venise on the Ionian island Corfu, that H.D. experienced a life-altering vision of projected "writing on the wall" in April 1920. She saw a sequence of forms so compelling and stymieing that she sought Freud's help in unraveling it: a soldier's head, a mystic chalice, a lamp in the form of the tripod at Delphi, a cluster of tiny creatures, the goddess Niké ascending an illuminated ladder, and a sun disk from which a man reached out to pull Niké into the light. Freud deemed the picture-writing a "dangerous symptom" and ultimately read it "as a desire for union with my mother," said H.D.[12] She was proud to present her images to Freud, to behold

11. H.D., *Notes on Thought and Vision* (San Francisco: City Lights, 1982), 26.

12. H.D., *Tribute*, 44.

the comingling of the poet and the psychoanalyst's researches and gifts. "Here is this hieroglyph of the unconscious or subconscious of the Professor's discovery and life-study, the hieroglyph in operation before our very eyes."[13]

I think of H.D. and Markopoulos as kindred protectors of the poetics of separation. They prevent overlap and merger between discrete images, and know the importance of singling out frames, symbols and colors in the process of divining, naming and re-ordering one's own objects, psychic and material. H.D. loved the semicircle of precious antiquities on Freud's desk, gods, goddesses and figurines, each a sharply-shaped representative of a unique mythological constellation; she was captivated by the idea of hieroglyphics—pictures that could be unlocked and hold their reliable forms at once. "I say,/take colour;/break white into red,/into blue/into violet/into green;/I say,/take each separately,/the white will slay," H.D. wrote in "Magician."[14] She called her poems "little boxes." (Pound called his failed early poems "stale creampuffs.")

And although the landscape around Lyssaraia is dry and brittle—covered in tall fawn-colored vegetation—it is full of discrete nuggets of moisture: honey, olives, grapes, figs, pears, plums, and blackberries. Stretches of bee boxes line the road, rows of brightly painted wooden cubes; and shrines, miniature steepled churches crowded with candles and icons, appear as mountainside markers of death. Markopoulos kept his *Eniaios* images separate, "little boxes" protected from each other by stretches of black and clear leader.

13. H.D., *Tribute*, 47.

14. H.D., "Magician," *Selected Poems* (New York: New Directions, 1988), 68.

"I say,/take colour;/break white into red,/into blue/
into violet/into green;/I say,/ take each separately,/
the white will slay," H.D. wrote in "Magician."

The overnight boat to Corfu offered a spectacle of sleeping arrangements: outdoors, on deck, bodies curled in frozen embrace with pets and children; indoors, in a communal room, spread blankets demarcated familial territory (it was crowded, though, so an oversized German couple and a gaggle of Italian model-types tolerated overlap); and private rooms featured lacquered green and red doors. At 4 a.m., I took a walk and discovered the back half of the boat was for rich people—a round, royal blue reception area led to flashy watch shops and all-night lounges. Near the stern I found a dirty porthole that looked out onto a house-size tangle of nautical materials, metals and knobs in every shade of orange and yellow. The churning of fresh, flat waves, produced over and over at a mechanical pace, surrounded the entire ship in a meter-thick border of foam.

I arrived at the Hotel Konstantinoupolis in Corfu Town at 8 a.m. and fell asleep immediately in a room permanently stamped with the memory of cigarettes. I dreamt that a boy announced: "a bed of stars."

In 1913, the Italian psychoanalyst Sandor Ferenczi wrote to Freud from the Grand Hotel D'Angleterre et Belle Venise in Corfu, where H.D. saw wall projections seven years later. He'd been struggling with sleeping disorders but his cure was underway. "More than half of my stay in Corfu is over, and I think I can affirm from now on that I can successfully take home a quite considerable reinvigoration as well as the conviction that my nightly sleep disturbances will have to be ameliorated by an intervention on the turbinate bones of my nose. I was naturally much more receptive to the beauties of the island on the days which followed nights on which I slept well. I thought of you countless times and wished I could have enjoyed, in an accustomed manner by your side, the beauties…"[15]

"[T]here is no faith and no hope/without sleep," H.D. wrote in "Magician." She incubated famously for curative purposes—on the Scilly Isles off the coast of Cornwall in 1919, where she healed from a constellation of war-time traumas (the deaths of her brother and father and the dangerous labor she survived while giving birth to daughter Perdita) and produced the aphoristic *Notes on Thought and Vision*; in the Corfu hotel room, where she saw writing on the wall; and at 19 Berggasse in Vienna, where she reclined on Freud's couch five times a week in 1933 and 1934 during two series of psychoanalysis. H.D. dedicated her recollection of the Vienna period, *Writing on the Wall*, to "SIGMUND FREUD, *blameless physician*," borrowing Homer's term for Asclepios from the *Iliad*.

Stilia at the four-star Hotel Bella Venezia on Zambeli Street was delighted by my interest in the hotel and, though she hadn't heard of Hilda Doolittle, pleased to learn of a noted American associated with Corfu. (She was also politely appalled that I was staying at the shabbier Konstantinopoulos: "I assume next time you'll be lodging here?") She regretted to inform me that H.D.'s Belle Venise had been destroyed, bombed by the Germans in 1943. As consolation, Stilia served me an iced Nescafé frappé and took a framed bill from the original hotel, soiled and torn, off the wall so I could inspect it. We toured the back gardens and she wrote down all the flower names: *jacaranda* (slender blue bells), *lantana* (clusters of red and orange florets), *hibiscus* (crepe paper blossoms). At the front reception desk, a single white rose floated in a low glass.

---

15. Eva Brabant et al., eds., *The Correspondence of Sigmund Freud and Sandor Ferenczi* (Cambridge: Belknap, 1994), 476.

Sandor Ferenczi wrote to Freud from the Grand Hotel D'Angleterre et Belle Venise: "More than half of my stay in Corfu is over, and I think I can affirm from now on that I can successfully take home a quite considerable reinvigoration as well as the conviction that my nightly sleep disturbances will have to be ameliorated by an intervention on the turbinate bones of my nose."

Flowers figured prominently in H.D.'s vision of intimate gift exchange, emblems of desire passed back and forth with those who shared her secret language and served as helpmates in her ongoing quest for accurate translation. "[V]iolets were laid on the pages of a paperbound copy of Euripedes' *Ion*, open on the table of my Corfu Hotel Belle Venise bedroom. It seemed a 'mystery' but Bryher"—the novelist Annie Winifred Ellerman, H.D.'s longtime companion and co-interpreter of the wall drawings—"must have left them," H.D. recalled in 1933.[16] She sent gardenias to Freud (his favorite) when he was in London exile in 1938; he offered her dark-leaved orange branches during one of their sessions.[17] In *Paint It Today*, H.D. recalled her mother's over-protection in the form of flowers: "she put morning glories through the string of every birthday parcel."[18]

Stilia remained hopeful: she sent me to the Corfu Literary Society to continue my search. I arrived and asked for the director, Mr. Papadatos; a man with an eye patch and a blue polo shirt paused and replied, expressionless, "you are speaking with him." The Literary Society would be of no use to me, he said. As I walked out I was heartened to discover a carved owl, the Society's emblem, on the front door. As a child, asked to keep quiet in her father's book-lined study (a room she identified with Freud's analytic room), H.D. was captivated by a stuffed snow-owl under a bell jar. In 1932, the painter Kenneth Macpherson—Bryher's gay husband and H.D.'s lover (the three operated as a family unit and together managed the film group POOL)—designed a bookplate for H.D. as a Christmas gift: an owl perched on a branch carved with her initials,

16. H.D., *Tribute*, 167.

17. Apparently Freud himself was not a strict Freudian.

18. H.D., *Paint it Today* (New York: NYU Press, 1992), 43.

encased in a dome of leaves. "The OWL is almost too occult to gaze at...I love it so," she said in gratitude.[19]

But I was vaguely ashamed of the literal—and in vain—approach I'd taken in my search for signs of H.D.'s presence on Corfu (had I expected the local news station to dig up archival footage of her "writing on the wall"?) and my naïve delight in finding shadows of her symbols. I took the owl on the Literary Society door as a sign: permission—to call off my search.[20] As H.D. plainly announced in *Notes on Thought and Vision*, "my sign-posts are not yours, but if I blaze my own trail, it may help to give you confidence ... to get out of the murky, dead world of overworked emotions and thoughts."[21]

THE SEA GARDEN [22]

Down the hill from the gardens, forests and Doric temple ruins of the Mon Repos estate just above Corfu Town, I found a tall succulent plant with a gray stalk, its branches tiny s-curve offerings, younger and pale green, on the edge of an empty beach. A cactus, a pine tree and an olive tree crowded around it, and all of the forms leaned above the water in perfectly-edged profile. Inside the woods, vegetation was dense and tropical—dead weeping palm leaves and waxy fans—and coniferous all at once. All of the best forms had been gathered into one frame: the desert and sea and the tropical and temperate.

---

19. Diana Collecott, "*Owl* note," in Michael King, ed., *H.D.: Woman and Poet* (Orono: National Poetry Foundation, 1986), 143.

20. When she could not locate Freud's favorite flowers, H.D. said, "but in imagination, at least, in the mist of a late afternoon, I could still continue a quest, a search. There might be gardenias somewhere." *Tribute*, 11.

21. H.D., *Notes*, 24.

22. The title of H.D.'s 1916 volume of poems: her first published book.

On the hilltop, the estate garden over-stimulated me; there was something intensely adorable (not *cute*, but worth loving) about it that I couldn't understand. It was not lush—but craggy, sharp, dry and old-fashioned. All the blooms were tight and tiny, the trees stout and arthritic. The roses were spaced far apart, rows bracketed by terra cotta scalloped tiles; every flower had plenty of room. A marigold-colored mess spread out on the ground, and a bright violet vine was speckled with red-petaled dots. The garden was the result of someone's vision. I thought of the filmmaker Marie Menken and the way she shot Dwight Ripley's Long Island garden in 1957, and saw for the first time what was required to make a film: show up with a movie camera, alone, in a place that makes you want to jump.

I had grown attached to a cloud of blossoms next to a hillside monastery in Order V of *Eniaios*, and decided later they were pink laurels, or rhododendrons. When I saw them again on both sides of a Mon Repos footpath, I tried to capture them with my camera but there was nothing to retrieve—just pixelated petal close-ups.

I followed the path to the end of the grounds. Back on the street, violet-fuchsia flowering bushes were pruned into a continuous row of arches. A bus of precisely the same color passed underneath, and Mon Repos was gone.

INTOLERABLE RADIUM[23]

In *Notes on Thought and Vision*, H.D. tells of Lo-fu, a Ming Dynasty poet who studied an apple branch with profound concentration

---

23. "I say,/worship each separate;/no man can endure/ your intolerable radium," H.D. wrote in "Magician."

until he had memorized its every turn and shade. "Then he went inside and in his little cool room out of the sun he closed his eyes. He saw that branch but more clearly, more vividly than ever. That branch was his mistress now, his love."[24]

When, far from the shore, I pushed my head out from underwater at Paleokastritsa (H.D. visited in 1920, just before the hotel vision), my eyes opened to the sight of a hilltop tree I knew well, a thin conical pine from the last hour of the final Temenos projection.[25] I imagine the *Eniaios* images I am left with as lifesavers: partially dissolved gem-like slivers, already inside. Like the colored rock candies that Jacques Rivette's Céline and Julie trade mouth-to-mouth, they are facilitators of time travel and reminders of old secrets. I am grateful for the separation among the images in *Eniaios* because now they are mine.

Markopoulos drew a line around a generous field in the creation of *Eniaios* and the Temenos, one that included not only his projected film reels but the place and the journey and every register of time, including sleep. As any good magician or psychoanalyst knows, it's the deliberate chalking of a particular square that allows for the discovery of personal order and private mythology. And hence, on my final night, in Athens, everything wrapped up. *Living Golf* on CNN featured a tournament in Crete: an update of my first dream about Markopoulos the TV producer blasting blossoming golf clubs into the sky. And that night, I dreamt of pouring soap into a small hole in the ground; then I rinsed off under a spigot. Perhaps this phase of purification was complete.

---

24. H.D., *Notes*, 44.

25. Beavers: "The projected film image reaches deeply. It can remain with the spectator and awaken thoughts long after the actual screening." Pipolo, 34.

10.

O

I imagine your trainer, Bob Greene, has an internal knot—on the one hand, he's Oprah's trainer, so that opens up product and marketing opportunities, and on the other, he has no authority: you haven't kept the weight off.

At a certain point I said to him, "Bob, you have my blessing if you want to go. But I would love to be able to continue giving you baskets of my favorite things if you stay."

But "Oprah's Favorite Things" are geared toward women, aren't they?

Stedman lives in the merino-cashmere slipper socks when we're in Vail. They have rubber traction—they're like a deconstructed driving moccasin. I don't know why it's so hard for us to accept that our men need swaddling too.

Stedman's a baby?

No. And neither were Oprah's viewers. Someone like Ellen gives baby gifts to celebrities—as if Sarah Michelle Gellar needs a rococo bassinet *gratis*. It's called overcompensating for being a lesbian.

Top: Artist Pawel Wojtasik's bathroom, Brooklyn, NY.
Bottom: Women's bathroom, New York Psychoanalytic Society.

Gayle always said I should tuck a few of my karma points into the gift baskets—I've given away so much that my own basket is overflowing.

When you lost all that weight in 1988, you pulled a red wagon with 67 pounds of fat onto the stage wearing a black turtleneck sweater tucked into Calvin Klein jeans.

I was thrilled that I had drunk myself skinny with Optifast in four months. I wanted each episode to be worth a year of therapy for my viewers.

So the fat was like Sean Landers' 451 page hand-written memoir *[sic]*—if it had been rendered in lard and had no words?

I would have respected Sean's piece a lot more if he'd started it off with "Dear Mom" or "Dear Ann Landers" and then dropped it in the mail and waited quietly for a reply. Sometimes if you can find a celebrity with your own name you don't have to become one.

But you didn't lose 67 pounds of actual fat. Weight loss is 30% water.

A couple of days before we did the ribbon-cutting at Harpo Productions in Chicago, I sat with Alan Greenspan in his apartment in Georgetown. It's elegant—it has a high-end soap opera aesthetic with floating slate stairs and an overall taupe and steel blue ambiance, like *As the World Turns*. I can see why Andrea Mitchell came over for a drink after their first date and essentially never left. I signed a contract, more or less saying that when in doubt I'd err on the side of the interests of free market capitalism. Phil Donahue had given me Alan's contact—he said it was like going for a few sessions of couples counseling before getting married. So it was a compromise I made with my eyes open. And then we toasted with some 1787 Château Margaux.

Does Alan attend Jeffrey Goldberg's D.C. Torah study group with David Brooks and David Gregory?

No. Alan davens alone. He said to think of capitalism as a golden rod—keep bending it as far as you can, but when the metallic surface starts to crack and flake off (it's spray-painted gold), you've got to back off so others can keep using it. He said, "Oprah, you're our Wounded Healer: maintain a low-grade infection without going into sepsis." I had to promise to foreswear therapy as long as *The Oprah Show* was on the air to keep the wound moist and protect the brand.

Was Andrea around when you were at the apartment?

No. She and Candice Bergen were meeting for lunch for the first time since they were classmates at Penn. After Louis Malle got sick and Andrea went blonde, the power dynamic between them finally gave way.

I spent Career Day in high school with Mona Scott at WCMH in Columbus. She was blonde and it turned out we had the same lambswool charcoal-colored cardigan from Benetton. She was married to Doug Adair and they co-anchored the local news.

You'll be hard pressed to find a female newscaster who isn't married. The gift economy of seated TV journalism is off the charts.

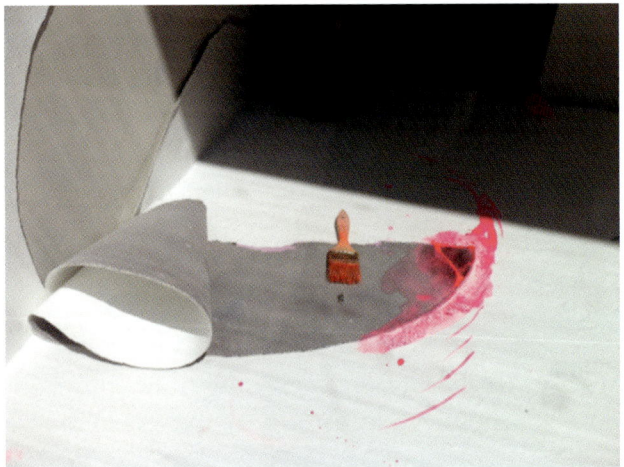

Top: *The Fathers of the Church*, Labyrinth Books, Princeton, NJ.
Bottom: Window display, ABC Carpet & Home, New York, NY.

Top: Fabric swatches for the Chapel of the Rosary at Vence.
Bottom: Sister Jacques-Marie responds to "Was Matisse in love
with you?"

But you and Stedman didn't marry.

I knew I was taking a risk by walking around *en plain air* on *The Oprah Winfrey Show*. Whenever I watch Diane Sawyer, I think, wow—you won the lottery. The rushing around to meet world leaders in pants over hose, skimming the producer's notes in a plush leather binder on the way to the UN, cackling with Mike Nichols at night, bothering to stock up on kefir for fruit smoothies so her gut doesn't leak on the weekends. The way she leans forward in the chair, savoring the outpouring of words: this is as close as you can get to being present while remaining totally blind.

It's sort of like walking around the perimeter of Serra's *Torqued Ellipses*, as close as you can get without touching the rusty steel. You get to make contact with an ideal mother and father all at once—there's both gentle recognition and the spirit of unwavering authority. You passively follow the line of his torque and get rewarded by an internal liveliness.

Serra needs your body as much as you need his. But it's difficult. By the time you learn to read the news properly—to be in control of the rhythm of delivery, and then master enough of the information so that you don't get caught in an embarrassing situation— there's not a lot of subjectivity left over. You have to report on Dick Cheney's heart transplant, be competent about the technology and the surgical terms, keep the diction fluid and the affect consistent and in the meantime you've had to get a sitter in order to be able to report from Walter Reed before the surgeons arrive to scrub up at 5 a.m. Being a newscaster is basically feeling grateful for the self-ordering and access to language that come from lending your body and mind to supporting the establishment and then

Top: Braves coach Bobby Cox, Baseball Hall of Fame,
Cooperstown, NY.
Bottom: Dressing room door, Urban Outfitters, New York, NY.

converting that gratitude into forms of care and kindness that can't be argued with.

But don't forget that the chair is padded. Even though you're wearing something uncomfortable, you feel contained, and because of hair and makeup there's a kind of rightness about extending into space. Your nails and lashes lead the way. The fact that your hair doesn't move when you do gives you a sense of the best kind of female citizenship. And then when you have spontaneous moments—like everyone gangs up on the weather guy or there's some unintended sexual pun—the gratification is over the top. You get to manage authority and play in a space of seconds, and that combined with the lights and the crew—you just feel happy to be alive.

Is sounds like Michael Balint's patient who did a somersault in the middle of a session.

No. That was a full-bodied gesture of non-compliance, available to a basic fault patient for representation strictly in the therapeutic environment. That patient had been lying down. The spontaneity I'm talking about takes place within the context of the phallic swap-mart of TV. In the chair.

Children returning from an island, Paris, France.

ABOUT THE AUTHOR

Rebekah Rutkoff is a New York-based writer and artist. Her work has appeared in publications including *Artforum*, *Fence*, *Animal Shelter*, *Framework* and *World Picture Journal* and she has exhibited and programmed moving image work internationally. She is the recipient of grants and fellowships from the Creative Capital | Warhol Foundation Arts Writers Grant Program, the Onassis Foundation and Princeton University. She is the editor of a book about the filmmaker Robert Beavers forthcoming from the Austrian Film Museum/Columbia University Press.